Improve your aural! Grade 1

Paul Harris and John Lenehan

Contents

fabermusic.com

© 2006 by Faber Music Ltd
First published in 2006 by Faber Music Ltd.
Updated edition first published in 2011
Bloomsbury House 74–77 Great Russell Street London WC1B 3DA
Music processed by Music Set 2000
Design by Susan Clarke
Illustrations on page 9 by Drew Hillier
Printed in England by Caligraving Ltd
All rights reserved

ISBN10: 0-571-53438-4
EAN13: 978-0-571-53438-8

CD recorded in Rectory Studio, High Wycombe, March 2006
Created and produced by John Lenehan
Thanks to Godstowe School Chamber Choir 2006 and Laurel Hopkinson
℗ 2006 Faber Music Ltd
© 2006 Faber Music Ltd

Why is aural important?

You may wonder why you have to do aural at all. The answer is, that aural will help you improve as a musician. And this may surprise you – it will help perhaps more than *any other* single musical skill.

Aural is all about understanding and processing music that you hear and see, in your head. By doing so, you will find that your own playing improves enormously. You will be able to play more expressively and stylistically, be more sensitive to quality and control of tone, your music reading will improve, you will be able to spot your own mistakes, be more sensitive to others when playing or singing in an ensemble, be more aware of intonation, improve your ability to memorise music and improve your ability to improvise and compose.

All the many elements of musical training are of course connected. So, when working through the activities in this book you will be connecting with many of them. You'll be listening, singing, clapping, playing your instrument, writing music down, improvising and composing – as well as developing that vital ability to do well at the aural tests in your grade exams!

Aural is not an occasional optional extra – just to be taken off a dusty shelf a few days (or even hours) before a music exam. It's something you can be developing and thinking about all the time. And as you go through the enjoyable and fun activities in these books you'll realise how important and useful having a good musical ear (being good at aural) really is.

How to use this book

When you have a few minutes to spare (perhaps at the beginning or end of a practice session), sit down with your instrument, by your CD player, and open this book. Choose a section and then work through the activities – you needn't do much each time. But whatever you do, do it carefully, repeating any activity if you feel it will help. In fact many of the activities will be fun to do again and again. And make sure that you come back to the book on a regular basis.

So, good luck and enjoy improving your aural skills!

Paul Harris and John Lenehan

For U.S. readers:
Bar = Measure
Note = Tone
Tone = Whole step

Section 1 Pulse

Pulse is the heartbeat of music. It divides time into regular and equal units. Go for a walk taking short, even and regular steps. Listen to a clock ticking or watch a pendulum swinging; listen to a washing machine or a dishwasher – these are all examples of pulse.

● Pulse is all around us. How many other kinds of pulse can you think of?

● This is a steady pulse. Walk round the room (or on the spot) to the pulse. After you've finished listening to the track, continue to hear the pulse in your head.

Pulse can be grouped into patterns of two or more. (Each individual pulse is normally called a beat).

● This is a pulse in 2-time. Clap along with it.

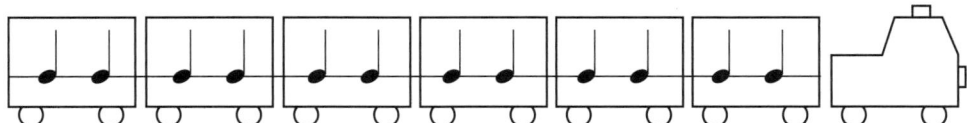

● This is a pulse in 3-time. Clap along with it.

When writing music down, each group is divided by a bar-line and the space between each bar-line is called a bar.

● Put in the bar-lines:

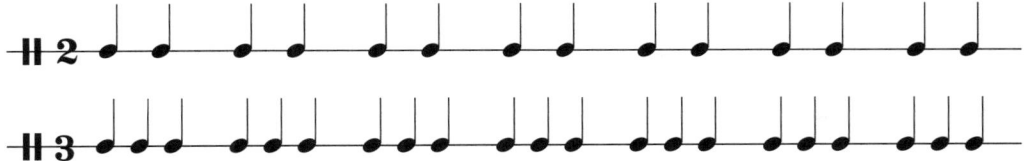

listening activities

track 5

1 Clap along with the pulse, joining in as soon as you can. From time to time the pulse on the recording will stop. Keep going steadily and evenly all the time, until you hear the whistle.

track 6

2 This time, instead of clapping the pulse out loud, hear it in your head.

track 7

3 In this example, there is a lot more silence. Continue clapping the pulse throughout the track. Are you precisely with the pulse each time it returns?

track 8

4 This time hear the pulse in your head. Are you precisely with the pulse each time it returns?

track 9

5 In this exercise the pulse is 4-in-a-bar. After two introductory bars, one beat in each bar is missed out (the same one each time). Clap only the missing beat. Which beat is it?

track 10

6 Here's a similar exercise but this time in 3-in-a-bar. Again clap the missing beat. Which beat is it?

track 11

7 Here's an exercise to help you develop your own inner sense of pulse. You'll hear three bars of a pulse in 2-time with counting, and then it will stop. Continue counting on your own and silently in your head. In which bar and on which beat does the sound occur? What is the sound?

track 12

8 Here's a similar example in 3-time. In which bar and on which beat does the sound occur? This time the sound is played by an instrument. Can you tell which one?

track 13

9 Here are four examples of music in 2-time. Clap (or tap) the pulse, joining in as soon as you can.

track 14

10 Here are four more examples, now in 3-time. Again, clap (or tap) the pulse, joining in as soon as you can.

track 15

11 Clap (or tap) the pulse of each of the musical excerpts on this track, joining in as soon as you can. After each one, write down whether it was in 2-time or 3-time.

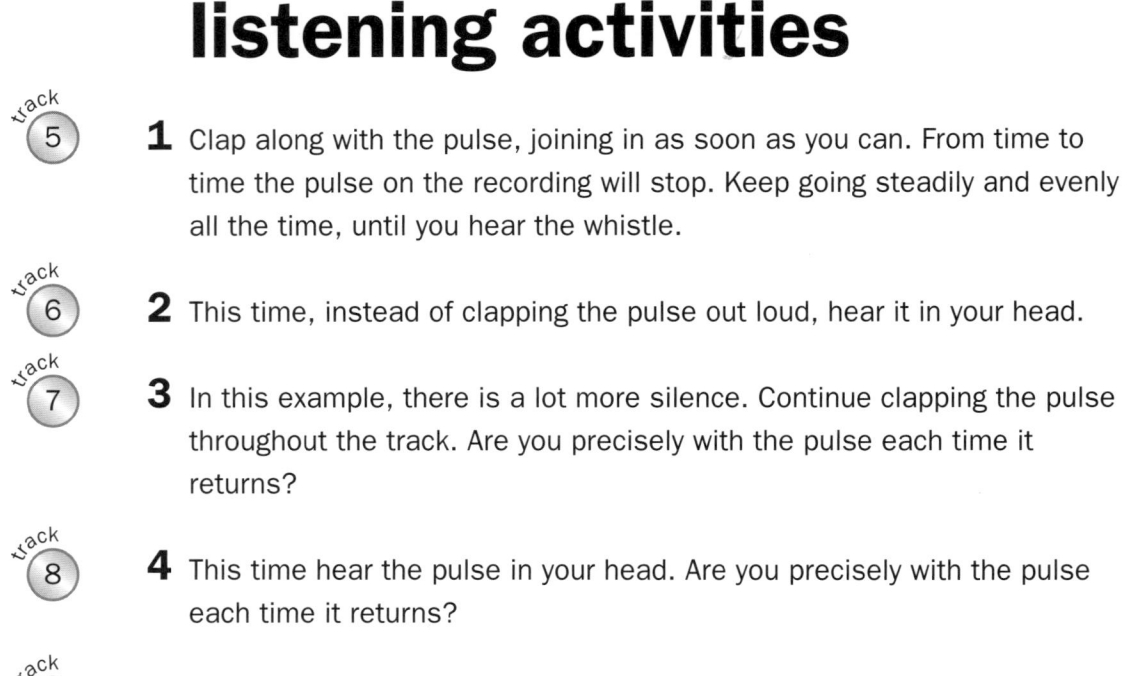

1 $\frac{3}{4}$ ✓   2 $\frac{2}{4}$ ✓   3 $\frac{2}{4}$ ✓   4 $\frac{3}{4}$ ✓   5 $\frac{3}{4}$ ✗ $\frac{2}{4}$

12 In this exercise you'll hear a series of short rhythmic phrases in 2-time over a steady pulse. Clap or tap each one back straight away like an echo. The first one is done for you.

13 Here are some more exercises, now in 3-time. Again the first one is done for you.

14 This time, instead of repeating the rhythm, improvise your own rhythmic responses.

15 Listen to the phrase which will be repeated four times. Write down the rhythm on the line below:

16 Now here's an example in 3-time. Listen to the phrase (repeated four times) and then write down the rhythm:

17 Ask your teacher to play you one of the pieces you are learning. Clap or tap the pulse. How many beats in the bar?

18 Using a piece you are currently working on, hear the first four bars in your head. Now, without the music, have a go at answering the following questions:

- How many beats are there in each bar? _____
- What are the time values of the first two notes of the tune? _____
- Are there any rests in the first four bars? _____
- If so, what are they? _____
- Hear the first four bars in your head and at the same time tap the pulse.
- Now hear the pulse in your head and tap the rhythm.
- Write down the rhythm of the melody of the first four bars. Put in the time signature:

Come back and repeat this exercise using other pieces or using other four-bar phrases from the same piece.

Section 2 Pitch

● Sing the highest note you can (comfortably) – and now the lowest. Now sing some of the notes in between.

Each of these notes is a different 'pitch'. Pitch is how high or low a sound seems. Some notes are 'high-pitched' and others are 'low-pitched'.

● Go to a piano or electric keyboard (or use your instrument if you don't have access to one of these) and sing a comfortable high note. Now try to find it on the instrument. Now do the same with a low note. How far apart are your highest and lowest notes? Is it more than one octave?

Like pulse, pitch is also all around us. Can you think of some high- and low-pitched animal sounds? For example, birdsong is usually high in pitch and a lion's roar is quite low in pitch. How would you describe the pitch of the following?

● A door creaking

● Your door bell

● The ringtone of your phone

● A car engine

Now listen to the three pieces on track 21. One is high-pitched (H), one medium- (M) and one low- (L). Put them in the correct order.

1 ___M___ ✓   2 ___L___ ✓   3 ___H___ ✓

Getting to know your voice

● Play a note on the piano (or on your instrument) in the middle of your range. Listen to it very carefully and then hear it in your head like a gentle hum.

● Now hear the hum get louder, still in your head. Now begin to hum the note out loud very quietly. Gradually get louder. You've successfully pitched a note. Repeat this many times using different notes.

● Now play two next-door notes, one after the other. Hear them in your head and then hum or sing them out loud to *lah* or any other sound. Repeat this many times using different pairs of notes.

● Sing a phrase from a piece you are studying. Get into the habit of singing, at least a few notes, every day.

listening activities

track 22 **1** A series of notes can move in three different ways – they can stay the same, go up or go down. On this track, you'll hear some two-note phrases. Some go up (U), some go down (D) and some stay the same (S). Now listen to the five phrases and write down the letters U, D or S after you've heard each one:

1 _D͟X͟U͟_ 2 _S͟ ✓_ 3 _U͟X͟D͟_ 4 _U͟ ✓_ 5 _S͟ ✓_

track 23 **2** Now you'll hear the example again. This time you will be given longer pauses between each phrase for you to write the shape down. Here's how the first one should look:

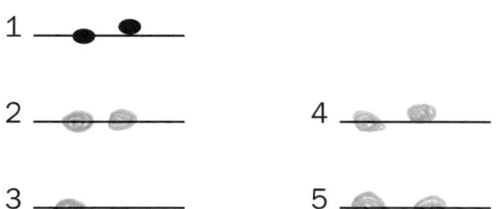

track 24 **3** Here are the same notes again. This time sing each two-note pattern after you've heard it. The first one is sung for you.

track 25 **4** Now, with your instrument, play the notes after you've heard them. The first note is a concert C. Begin on any suitable octave. (B♭ instruments begin on D; E♭ instruments begin on A.)

track 26 **5** On this track there are five short phrases. Sing each phrase as soon as you've heard it. The first one is sung for you.

tracks 27-30 **6** On these four tracks you'll hear some more phrases. Follow the instructions on the CD.

7 Now have a go at making up your own short phrases using the notes C, D and E. Write them down, then hear them in your head, then sing them and then finally play them.

1

2

3

4

8 Working with a friend, try playing your tunes from the previous exercise. Ask your friend to sing and play them back to you.

tracks 31-36

9 Here are some more short phrases. Sing each one back as soon as you've heard it.

10 Using a piece you are currently working on, find a suitable two-bar phrase and try to answer the following questions:

• How many different pitches are there in the phrase? _____

• Are any notes repeated? _____

• What is the name of the first note? _____

• Play the first note and then hear the phrase in your head.

• Now sing the phrase, firstly looking at the notes and then again from memory.

• Now, from memory, write the phrase down.

Paul Harris's Exam Workout!

IMPROVE YOUR SIGHT-READING!

The ability to sight-read fluently is an important part of musical training, whether intending to play professionally, or simply for enjoyment. By becoming a good sight-reader, the player will be able to learn pieces more quickly, pianists will accompany more easily and all musicians will play duets and chamber music with confidence and assurance. Also, in grade examinations, a good performance in the sight-reading test will result in useful extra marks!

Improve your sight-reading! is a series of workbooks designed to help incorporate sight-reading regularly into practice and lessons, and to help prepare for the sight-reading test in grade examinations. It offers a progressive series of enjoyable and stimulating stages which, with careful work, should result in considerable improvement from week to week.

Step by step, the player is encouraged to build up a complete picture of each piece. Rhythmic exercises help develop and maintain a steady beat, whilst melodic exercises assist in the recognition of melodic shapes at a glance. The study of a prepared piece with associated questions for the student to answer helps consolidate acquired skills and, finally, the real, unprepared sight-reading test itself. Mark-boxes for each stage help keep a check on progress.

Such practical and methodical material is guaranteed to take the horror out of sight-reading!

0-571-53300-0	Piano Pre-Grade 1	NEW EDITION
0-571-53301-9	Piano Grade 1	NEW EDITION
0-571-53302-7	Piano Grade 2	NEW EDITION
0-571-53303-5	Piano Grade 3	NEW EDITION
0-571-53304-3	Piano Grade 4	NEW EDITION
0-571-53305-1	Piano Grade 5	NEW EDITION
0-571-53306-X	Piano Grade 6	NEW EDITION
0-571-53307-8	Piano Grade 7	NEW EDITION
0-571-53308-6	Piano Grade 8	NEW EDITION
0-571-51385-9	Violin Grade 1	
0-571-51386-7	Violin Grade 2	
0-571-51387-5	Violin Grade 3	
0-571-51388-3	Violin Grade 4	
0-571-51389-1	Violin Grade 5	
0-571-51735-8	Violin Grade 6	
0-571-51736-6	Violin Grade 7–8	
0-571-51075-2	Viola Grades 1–5	

0-571-51873-7	Cello Grades 1–3
0-571-51874-5	Cello Grades 4–5
0-571-51149-X	Double Bass Grades 1–5
0-571-51373-5	Descant Recorder Grades 1–3
0-571-51466-9	Flute Grades 1–3
0-571-51467-7	Flute Grades 4–5
0-571-51789-7	Flute Grade 6
0-571-51790-0	Flute Grades 7–8
0-571-51464-2	Clarinet Grades 1–3
0-571-51465-0	Clarinet Grades 4–5
0-571-51787-0	Clarinet Grade 6
0-571-51788-9	Clarinet Grades 7–8
0-571-51635-1	Saxophone Grades 1–3
0-571-51636-X	Saxophone Grades 4–5
0-571-51633-5	Oboe Grades 1–3
0-571-57021-6	Oboe Grades 4–5
0-571-51148-1	Bassoon Grades 1–5
0-571-51076-0	Horn Grades 1–5
0-571-50989-4	Trumpet Grades 1–5
0-571-51152-X	Trumpet Grades 5–8
0-571-56860-2	Trombone Grades 1–5

IMPROVE YOUR AURAL!

The very thought of aural, especially in examinations, strikes fear into the heart of many young pianists and instrumentalists. But aural should not be an occasional optional extra – it's something to be developing all the time, because having a good ear will help improve musicianship more than any other single musical skill.

Improve your aural! is designed to take the fear out of aural. Through fun listening activities, boxes to fill in and practice exercises, these workbooks and CDs focus on all the elements of the ABRSM aural tests. Because all aspects of musical training are of course connected, the student will also be singing, clapping, playing their instrument, writing music down, improvising and composing – as well as developing that vital ability to do well at the aural test in your grade exams!

0-571-53438-4	Grade 1 (with CD)	NEW EDITION
0-571-53439-2	Grade 2 (with CD)	NEW EDITION
0-571-53544-5	Grade 3 (with CD)	NEW EDITION
0-571-53545-3	Grade 4 (with CD)	NEW EDITION
0-571-53546-1	Grade 5 (with CD)	NEW EDITION
0-571-53440-6	Grade 6 (with CD)	NEW EDITION
0-571-53441-4	Grades 7–8 (with CD)	NEW EDITION

IMPROVE YOUR PRACTICE!

Improve your practice! is the essential companion for pianists, encapsulating Paul Harris's failsafe approach to learning.

With boxes for filling in, make-your-own playing cards, a handy practice diary and, when needed, an exam countdown, these books help to explore the pieces and to understand their character. The books will enable the student to develop ways of getting the most out of their practice sessions – whatever their length.

Most importantly, the wider musical skills such as aural, theory, sight-reading, improvisation and composition develop alongside, resulting in a more intelligent and all-round musician. Practice makes perfect!

0-571-52844-9	Piano Beginners
0-571-52261-0	Piano Grade 1
0-571-52262-9	Piano Grade 2
0-571-52263-7	Piano Grade 3
0-571-52264-5	Piano Grade 4
0-571-52265-3	Piano Grade 5
0-571-52271-8	Instrumental Grade 1
0-571-52272-6	Instrumental Grade 2
0-571-52273-4	Instrumental Grade 3
0-571-52274-2	Instrumental Grade 4
0-571-52275-0	Instrumental Grade 5

IMPROVE YOUR TEACHING!

Energising and inspirational, **Improve your teaching!** and **Teaching Beginners** are 'must have' handbooks for all instrumental and singing teachers. Packed full of comprehensive advice and practical strategies, they offer creative yet accessible solutions to the challenges faced in music education.

These insightful volumes are distilled from years of personal experience and research. In his approachable style, Paul Harris outlines his innovative strategy of 'simultaneous learning' as well as offering advice on lesson preparation, aural and memory work, effective practice and more.

0-571-52534-2	Improve your teaching!
0-571-53175-X	Improve your teaching! Teaching beginners
0-571-53319-1	Group Music Teaching in Practice (with ECD)

IMPROVE YOUR SCALES!

Paul Harris's **Improve your scales!** is the only way to learn scales.

The purpose of the workbooks is to incorporate regular scale playing into lessons and daily practice, and to help pupils prepare for grade examinations. Each volume contains all the scales, arpeggios and ranges required for the relevant Associated Board exam, along with complementary practical material. 'Know your notes!' makes sure the actual notes *are* known!; 'finger fitness' exercises strengthen fingers and cover technically tricky areas and the scales, arpeggios and broken chord study pieces place the material in a more musical context. Simple improvisations and even an opportunity to 'have a go' at composing a short tune encourage thought 'in the key'.

This unique approach encourages the student to understand and play comfortably within in a key, thus helping them pick up those valuable extra marks in exams, as well as promoting a solid basis for the learning of repertoire and for sight-reading.

0-571-53411-2	Piano Grade 1	NEW EDITION
0-571-53412-0	Piano Grade 2	NEW EDITION
0-571-53413-9	Piano Grade 3	NEW EDITION
0-571-53414-7	Piano Grade 4	NEW EDITION
0-571-53415-5	Piano Grade 5	NEW EDITION
0-571-51664-5	Violin Grade 3	
0-571-51665-3	Violin Grade 4	
0-571-51666-1	Violin Grade 5	
0-571-51663-7	Violin Grades 1–2	
0-571-52024-3	Flute Grades 1–3	
0-571-52025-1	Flute Grades 4–5	
0-571-51475-8	Clarinet Grades 1–3	
0-571-51476-6	Clarinet Grades 4–5	

Faber Music Limited
Burnt Mill, Elizabeth Way, Harlow, Essex CM20 2HX. Tel: +44 (0)1279 828982 Fax: +44 (0)1279 828983
www.fabermusic.com

Hearing changes

● Have a look at these pictures and try to spot the eight differences:

That wasn't too difficult! Hearing the difference between two musical phrases is not difficult either. You just have to be very awake because it has to be done from memory, and it all happens in a very short time.

● Cover up the right-hand picture below. Now look at the picture on the left and study it for about 30 seconds.

● Now swap – cover up the left-hand picture and study the one on the right. Try to spot the differences *without looking back at the first picture.*

Not quite so easy, because you have to really remember the first picture. This is similar to the way you have to think when hearing changes in musical phrases – it's all in the memory …

listening activities

In the exam, you'll hear a phrase which, when repeated, will have a note changed. The new note will be either higher or lower than the original and the change will come either at the beginning (one of the first two notes) or at the end (one of the final two notes).

1 Remember, in any two-note phrase, the second note can do one of three things. It can stay the same, go higher (up in pitch) or go lower (down in pitch). In each two-note phrase on this track, write down whether the second note is higher (H), lower (L) or stays the same (S).

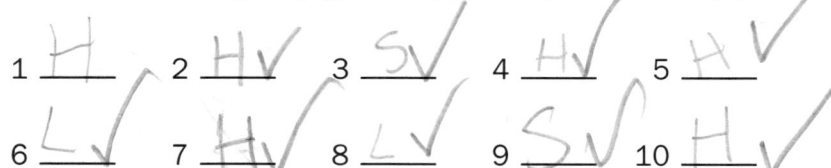

1 H   2 H   3 S   4 H   5 H
6 L   7 H   8 L   9 S   10 H

2 You'll hear four notes played twice in each of these exercises. In the second playing, one note will be changed. Simply write down which number note was changed (1, 2, 3 or 4).

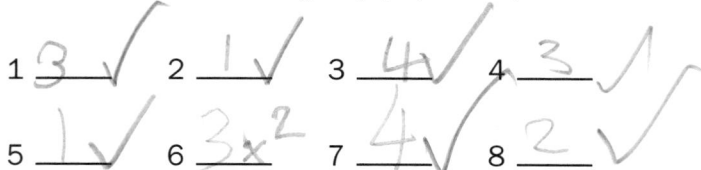

1 3   2 1   3 4   4 3
5 1   6 3x²   7 4   8 2

3 You'll hear some two-bar phrases in 3-time on this track. The second playing will have a change near the beginning (B) or near the end (E). Write down where you heard the change (B or E).

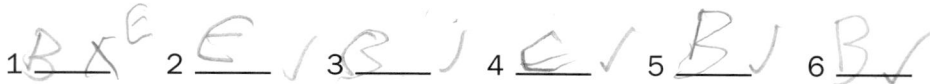

1 B x E   2 E   3 B   4 E   5 B   6 B

4 Now listen to track 39 again and this time write down whether the changed note was higher or lower.

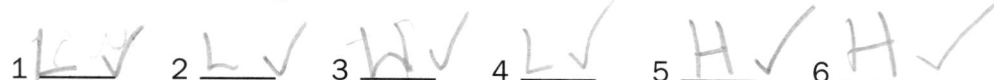

1 L   2 L   3 H   4 L   5 H   6 H

10

5 Now you'll hear some two-bar phrases in 4-time – again the second playing will have a change either near the beginning or near the end. Write down where you heard the change (B or E).

1 _B_ 2 _E_ 3 _B_ 4 _E_ 5 _E_ 6 _B_

6 Now listen to track 40 again and this time write down whether the changed note was higher or lower.

1 _higher_ 2 _higher_ 3 _lower_ 4 _higher_ 5 _higher_ 6 _lower_

7 Below you'll see a well-known carol. Firstly, reading the music, hear the piece through in your head. On the recording the pianist has made some mistakes! As you listen to the track, put a tick above the notes that have been played incorrectly. Listen again if you need to.

Section 4 Learning to listen to music

Learning to listen carefully to yourself and to other people playing music will help you improve your playing enormously. There are all sorts of features to listen out for, but for the Grade 1 exam you will only have to think about *dynamics* (loud and quiet playing) and *articulation* (smooth and detached playing).

From the moment you get up in the morning there will be many times when you hear music. Always take the opportunity to ask yourself some questions about it:

- Is the music loud (*forte*) or quiet (*piano*)?
- Is the music detached (*staccato*) or smooth (*legato*)?
- Does the music gradually get louder (*crescendo*) or quieter (*diminuendo*)?
- What instruments are playing?

listening activities

 track 42

1 As you listen to each of the three short pieces on this track, write down *f* (*forte*) for the loud sections and *p* (*piano*) for the quiet sections.

1 ___P___ ___F___ ✓

2 ___P___ ___F___ ___P___ ✓

3 ___F___ ___P___ ___F___ ___P___ ✓

 track 43

2 As you listen to each of the three short pieces on this track, write down L (*legato*) for the smooth sections and S (*staccato*) for the detached sections.

1 ___L___ ___S___ ✓

2 ___S___ ___L___ ___S___ ✓

3 ___L___ ___S___ ___L___ ✓

 track 44

3 Now write down 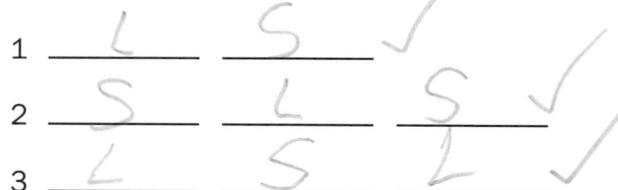 (*crescendo*) or (*diminuendo*) as you hear them.

1 ___<___ ___>___ ✓

2 ___<___ ___>___ ✗✗

3 ___>___ ___<___ ___>___ ✓

4 The next five tracks each contain a short piece. Each piece will be played twice. After the second playing, answer the following question:

track 45

- Did the piece begin loudly?

  _No_

track 46

- Was the end louder than the start?

  Yes

track 47

- Was the smooth section at the beginning or the end?

  end

track 48

- Where was the detached playing?

  _en d___

track 49

- Were the changes from quiet to loud sudden or gradual?

  Sudden

5 This time each piece is played only once and then you'll hear the questions:

track 50

- _Yes ✓ end x middle_

track 51

- _No   begining ✓_

track 52

- _____

track 53

- _____

track 54

- _____

6 Using a piece you are currently working on, try the following*:

- Add more dynamic markings (in pencil) and perform the piece to your teacher. Can your teacher hear all your extra dynamics?

- Play the piece ignoring all the markings!

- Play the piece really exaggerating all the markings!

- Play the piece reversing all the dynamic markings (eg. p = f, cresc. = dim. etc.)

- Play the smooth sections staccato and the detached sections smoothly or, if the piece is mostly smooth, play it staccato and if it's mostly detached, play it all smoothly.

*See *Improve your practice!* Grade 1 for more activities like this

Section 5 Making connections

These fun activities show you how aural connects with all the other aspects of music. Choose one or two each time you practise.

... with scales

Play the first note of a major scale you know well and then hear it in your head. Now play the scale very slowly, pre-hearing each note in your head *before* you play it.

... with tone quality

Listening to the *quality* of sound you make is very much part of aural. Choose a piece you are currently learning and play the first note (or, if it's a piano piece, the first chord or notes of both hands together) with the best tone quality you can.

... with intervals

Play a note and then, in your head, hear the note a tone (or major second) above (for example, play C and then hear D). Then play the note to see how accurate you were. Try to find some examples of tones in the pieces you are currently studying.

... with sight-reading

Choose a sight-reading piece* and try to hear it first in your head. Then play it.

... with memory

Choose a short phrase from a piece you are learning (two to four bars in length). Play it a few times, then, without the music, hear it in your head a few times and then play it from memory.

... with rhythm

Make up a four-bar rhythm in your head. Then write it down and clap it.

*For example from *Improve your sight-reading!* Grade 1

14

... with conducting

Listen to the theme tune to one of your favourite television programmes. What is the time signature? Ask your teacher how to beat time for that time signature and then conduct the music the next time you hear it.

... with music history

As a developing musician you will need to recognise the changing historical styles of music. Understanding style and musical periods will also help you to play your pieces with more conviction and authority. You'll hear four pieces, each from a different musical period. Using the descriptions, try to connect the boxes.

Baroque Slow dance in $\frac{3}{4}$	played 1st
Classical Sonata movement with lots of scale patterns	played 2nd
Romantic Character piece describing a storm	played 3rd
20th/21st century Pop-style ballad	played 4th

Composer's name:

A final message from the authors!

Answers

(by CD track number)

Section 1: *Pulse*

9   Third beat

10   Second beat

11   Bar 9, second beat – telephone

12   Bar 8, second beat – church organ

15   1:3, 2:2, 3:2, 4:3, 5:2

19

20

Section 2: *Pitch*

21   1:M, 2:L, 3:H

22   1:U, 2:S, 3:D, 4:U, 5:S

Section 3: *Hearing changes*

37   1:L, 2:H, 3:S, 4:H, 5:H, 6:L, 7:H, 8:L, 9:S, 10:H

38   1:3, 2:1, 3:4, 4:3, 5:1, 6:2, 7:4, 8:2

39   1:E, 2:E, 3:B, 4:E, 5:B, 6:B

     1:L, 2:L, 3:H, 4:L, 5:H, 6:H

40   1:B, 2:E, 3:B, 4:E, 5:E, 6:B

     1:L, 2:L, 3:H, 4:H, 5:L, 6:H

41

Section 4: *Learning to listen to music*

42   1: *p, f*   2: *p, f, p*   3: *f, p, f, p*

43   1: L, S   2: S, L, S   3: L, S, L

44   1: $<\,>$ 2: $>\,<$ 3: $>\,<\,>$

45   No

46   Yes

47   End

48   End

49   Sudden

50   Yes/Middle

51   No/Beginning

52   Staccato/No (ended loudly)

53   End/No (began loudly)

54   Sudden/*p*

Section 5: *Making connections*

55   The composer was BACH